Why you are here. Briefly

Why you are here.
Briefly

Nigel Linacre

BOOKS

Winchester, UK
Washington, USA

First published by O-Books, 2010
O Books is an imprint of John Hunt Publishing Ltd., The Bothy, Deershot Lodge, Park Lane, Ropley,
Hants, SO24 0BE, UK
office1@o-books.net
www.o-books.com

For distributor details and how to order please visit the 'Ordering' section on our website.

Text copyright: Nigel Linacre 2009

ISBN: 978 1 84694 349 2

A CIP catalogue record for this book is available from the British Library.

Design: Stuart Davies

Printed in the UK by CPI Antony Rowe
Printed in the USA by Offset Paperback Mfrs, Inc

Nigel Linacre

More vignettes at www.linacres.com

Feedback to info@linacres.com

Request talks - talk@linacres.com

Cofounder - www.xleadership.com

Cofounder - www.differi.com

Author, Recipes for Happiness

Who you are

Knowing

Why am I alive?

To find out why you are alive

What if I don't want to?

Then you won't

And once I find out?

New vistas will open

≈> You can understand what you don't

Opportunity

OK, I want to know who I am

Good, you can do that

Really?

Since you don't know who you are

How does that follow?

If you already knew, you couldn't find out

≈> Find out who you forgot you were

Who

Who am I?

Are you your hands or can you sense them?

I am someone who senses them

Are you your thoughts or feelings?

No, thoughts and feelings come and go

So who are you?

≈> Know yourself and that's it

Am I

Tell me who I am

You are being

Being what

Being conscious – and becoming

Becoming what?

Becoming who you are

≈> You are a human *becoming*

Me

I am consciousness?

Are you conscious?

Yes

You are consciousness

And if I'm not conscious?

Your response proves you are

≈> Consciousness is a means of experience; if you are

experiencing, you are conscious

Why

I want to know why I am here

Great, you are interested

How can I find out?

Turn these pages

≈> You will know what you know you can know

Point

What's the point of my life?

You don't know the point of your life?

That's why I am here

Then your point is to find your point

What if I don't want to?

You won't, until you do

≈> Until you know: the point is to find the point

Pointless

How do I know there's a point?

Suppose there's no point to anything

What?

Except for the point you choose

What's mine?

To keep your appointment

≈> While things may be pointless consciousness can be

single-pointed

Way

Show me the way?

There is no "the way"

So there is no way

There are many ways

How many?

As many ways as there are way-makers

≈> Make your own way one step at a time

Perfection

So why isn't the world perfect?

Suppose we could create a perfect world

That would be good

Then it would have to be imperfect first

≈> If perfection includes the process of creating perfection, it

includes imperfection

Imperfection

And how do I fit into all this?

You're imperfect too

So why am I here?

To become more perfect

≈> You are using this time to change yourself, or you aren't

Timing

And when will it become perfect?

We don't know

We don't know when?

When it is perfect there is nothing to know

≈> It turns out that everything you know is imperfect; in

perfection you lose every thing

Moments

There's no other reason to exist?

Each moment is experienced only if it exists

So what?

So you can enjoy every step of the journey

≈> Each moment is experienced only if it exists. Clearly, that is

what is happening right now

OK

How does the world work?

If you were in charge, how would it work?

It would be OK

Would you let people find out how it works?

Yes

You would have to let them forget first

≈> If you knew how the world works, you wouldn't be able to

find out

OK

The time of your life

Regrets

I regret the past

Is it done?

Yes

Can you undo it?

No

Why don't you forget it?

≈> The past is done and dusted

Past

I'm sad about what happened?

When did it happen?

In the past

Why are you still sad?

It made me

It's gone, it is no longer there, let it go

≈> None of the past is now real

Present

What is real now?

You are real now, or you could be

How could I be real?

You could let go of the past and the future

And then?

You could live in the present

≈> Resist the urge to cling to anything

Moments

I don't know what to do with my life

Try living

I don't know exactly what to do

Live each moment one at a time

How?

As though you are here now

≈> There's nowhere real to be but now

Now here

I don't know what will happen

And if you could see it all, how would you feel?

Overwhelmed

Enjoy life one moment at a time

≈ We sense a second at a time and a place at a time, though

the whole still is

Future

I worry about what might happen

When might it happen?

In the future

Why are you worried now?

What do you mean?

It isn't happening now

≈> All problems are in the fear and now

Sight

I'm nervous about the future

Realize the future does not exist

But it will do

You are confusing it with the present

I am still worried

Influence your imagination

≈> The future is imaginary

Go

So I can simply let go of the past?

When are you alive?

Well, now I suppose

And that's all the time you have

≈> Focus on who you are and what you are doing now, as now

is all you have

Now

Only now exists?

Yes

What about yesterday?

Now it's just memory

What about tomorrow?

Tomorrow is in embryo

≈> Freedom is now here

Seeing

I'd like to see the future

Then what would you do?

I'd already know

And the adventure would be over

≈> The drama comes from not knowing

Intent

I should stay in the present?

You can also go into the future

What's the point of that?

To make it up before it happens

How?

The future awaits your intentions

≈> Your imagination is your future factory

Pre-sent

Can I create the future?

You cannot not create the future

So I am creating the future

It is what you are doing in the present

How do I do it?

Consciously or unconsciously

≈> The future is pre-sent

No problem

Crisis

My life's a complete mess

Sounds like you are facing a crisis

Yes, that's right

Well that's good

Why!

In a crisis you have to grow

≈> Crises spur what the mundane didn't

Senseless

Life doesn't make sense

Until it does

But it's senseless

Expand your senses

How?

Practice

≈> If something makes no sense, your senses aren't getting it

Good

I'm not good enough

Good enough for what?

As good as I should be

Here's news: you're good enough for me

Thanks

And so is everyone else

≈> Without our judgment we are free to be ourselves

Make

Don't some things make you sad?

Sadness becomes a choice

Meaning?

Nothing makes me sad, as I control

What?

Myself

≈> Self-control is all you need

Confusion

I'm confused

Confusion's good

Why?

Because you are moving on

From what?

Old beliefs that no longer make sense

≈> Confusion comes when you get closer to new understanding

Wisdom

I don't know what to do

You could allow yourself to be led by wisdom

How do I do that?

What would wisdom do now?

⇝ Tune into the wisdom that is all around you: Start by getting

calm, then literally ask

Dialogue

This is a dialogue

With the universe

I thought we were talking

You are always talking to the universe

How?

Like that: and it is talking to you too

> The universe hears every thought you have; and it wants to

give you your next one

Done

I'm bad

You are wonderful right now

You don't know what I've done

I know what you're doing now

What's that?

Wondering

≈> The past constrains the present: until it doesn't

Forgiveness

I need forgiveness for what I've done

Who needs to forgive you?

Someone

Just one person can

Who's that?

Yourself, will you do that now?

≈> Forgiveness precedes love

Hook

What about other people's bad deeds?

Your response creates the stress you experience

You mean I'd better let them off

All of them for everything always

How will that help?

You'll feel better, they could feel loved

≈> Judgment damages the judge

Judge

I met a bad man

How do you know?

He did bad things

Why did he do what he did?

Don't know

So what do you know?

≈> Labelling doesn't change, love does

Forgive

Are you forgiving me?

One person's forgiveness works

Who is that?

Your: let yourself off the hook

≈> Forgive and you can live now here

Results

What results have you been getting in life?

Average

What do you expect?

More of the same

Is that the choice you want to make?

≈> Life is like a giant photocopier

Problem

Others judge me

Do they know you like you know you?

No, actually I judge me

And that's the problem

≈> You cannot judge others without judging yourself, and

neither can they

Fix

There are a lot of problems in the world

If we didn't have them we couldn't fix them?

Uh

Or even learn how to fix them

≈> Problems produce better results

Struggle

Life seems such a struggle

That is because you are struggling

But if I stop struggling I could lose

You could exchange the struggle

For what?

The flow

≈> What you struggle with, you empower

Travel

I'll feel better if I go somewhere else

Why would you?

I don't feel so good here

When you go, you'll still be there

≈> Circumstances change when you do: to change your

circumstances, change yourself

Sense and nonsense

Storm

How can I see clearly?

Your mind is like a storm

What can I do?

Let the storm subside, create some peace

Then what will I see?

Clearly

≈> To get peace of mind stop the storm

OK

What do I need to know?

That you are completely OK, just as you are

Is that all?

And so is everyone else

So I don't need to change?

And you don't need to change them

≈> Accept who you are and become who you weren't

Wonder

I often wonder

And then you stopped

If I keep wondering, I'll get it?

Keep wondering, and you'll sense wonder all around you

≈> Without wonder, life's not wonderful

Creative

How can I be creative?

Be open to receiving new thoughts

Don't I have to think them up?

No, just receive them

From where?

Beyond your consciousness

≈> Create some space for genius to flourish

Self

What can I take out of this world?

Can you take some possessions?

No

A physical body?

No, what then?

Your self

≈> Get to know yourself while you are still here

Short

Life's too short

You don't know how long it will be

A matter of years

That may be enough

For what?

That's up to you

≈> Over time, everything is a matter of choice

Wonder

This isn't such a wonderful life

Actually it's filled with wonder

That's not how it has seemed

Take time to experience it wonderfully

How do I do that?

Look around and wonder

≈> The wonder is how wonder isn't seen

Sense

Religion makes no sense to me

Why not rely on your senses?

How do you mean?

Sense the truth

But what if I haven't sensed it?

You have work to do

≈> Your senses can eliminate nonsense

Expand

How can I become more aware?

Expand your awareness

How can I do that?

Come to your senses

≈> Your senses are the key to knowing

5 Truth and Finding

Unknowing

I'd like to know

What would you like to know?

What I don't know

And how will you know it?

I don't know

≈> You will know once you will

Ready

If the truth is out there, why don't I know it already?

You didn't want to

So I can get to it now?

Yes, except it isn't out there

Where is it?

In here

≈> Truth is waiting for you to get into it

Truth

What's true?

What is?

But what is true?

What-is is what's true

How do you know?

You become it

≈> To recognize truth, adjust your wavelength

Where

If you know the truth, please tell it to me

It is all around you

How can I see it?

It is inside you too

Where?

Being

≈> The truth is what is: how could it be anything else?

Knowing

How do you know anything?

Don't know

If someone says it, do you know it?

Not sure

If you read it, do you know it?

Not sure

Then how do you know?

≈> You recognize what you already knew

Fragments

Do you know the truth?

No

Why not?

Because the truth is everything

Right, it is what is

We sense fragmentary moments

≈> The unknown truth is all that is

Wisdom

How can I become wise?

Know what you don't know

What don't I know?

You don't know anything

Where do I start?

By opening up

≈> See and hear more than you know

Source

Have you ever thought?

Thought what?

How thoughts get into your mind

Like that one?

And what you are thinking now

Where do they come from?

Else where

≈> Tune into where your thoughts form

Thoughts

Where do thoughts come from?

Don't know

Don't they just pop into your mind?

Sometimes yes

≈> Reach a thought just before it comes

Choice

Did I choose this life?

Why not?

What do you mean?

Why not choose this life?

≈> Sense yourself as a choice-maker

Believing

What should I believe?

Believe nothing

Nothing?

Instead of believing, know

How do you know?

Find out

≈> Beliefs are just temporary delusions

Mountain

When will I know the truth?

You'll know it when you are it

That sounds like a big mountain

Stop on a plateau

≈> Encouragement comes with each step

Seek

How can I find God?

Do you think God made everything?

Yes

Do you think God made you?

Yes

When you find your self you find God

≈> The creator is closer than your nose

Being alive

Exist

I think there's a reason why everything exists

What could that be?

I don't know

What would we miss if we didn't exist?

We wouldn't experience anything

Right

≈> Experience is the by-product of creation

Why

I know I'm here for a reason

Then you are

But I don't know what the reason is

What will you do?

Maybe I'll discover the reason

If that's what you want

≈> Persistent seeking becomes knowing

Awareness

Of what can I become aware?

What you have not been aware of

Why?

Then you will know what you don't

≈> If it is senseless, expand your senses

Need

What do people need to know?

They are absolutely OK exactly as they are

Then we wouldn't have to change

And that would make change easier

≈> You don't need to be or do anything

Others

What else do people need to know?

Others are absolutely OK exactly as they are

But then we wouldn't have to change anyone

Right, we could accept other people too

All conflict would be pointless

We could give up

≈> No-one else needs to be or do anything to be OK

Contribution

How can I make a really worthwhile contribution?

Focus on someone's growth

Whose?

Your own

Why mine?

The more you are, the more you can

≈> Stay the same and life stays the same

Guarantee

Does spiritual enquiry work?

Is anything guaranteed?

Are you asking me to take it on trust?

There is one way to find out

≈> Spiritual experiments produce results

Wanted

I need to be wanted

You need to know you are wanted

Who wants me?

You do, and try appreciating others

How will that help?

You'll forget what you didn't have

≈> Share what you don't have

Watching

It feels like I am changing

What you are conscious of is changing

Will I ever become unchanging?

Be conscious of what you are conscious

How will that help?

Then you can watch the storm from a cave

≈> Stop spending all your time watching out, and start to watch

in

People

I wish people weren't the way they are

You are confused about who you are not

Who am I not?

You are not them, you are yourself

OK, I can be myself

Change yourself

≈> You change yourself or you don't

Security

How can I feel secure?

How can you be sure you won't die tomorrow?

I'm not

The only way would be to die today

≈> There is no security in the world, save who you are

Experience

What do you really believe?

I don't believe, I experience

What do you experience?

This moment

Anything else?

And this one

≈> The extraordinary experience is being

Outside in

Rich

I'll be happy when I'm rich

Why do people want to be rich?

They want to feel different

And that's because they're unhappy

≈> Happiness is immaterial

More

I'll feel better if I have more stuff

Why would you?

I'll feel more secure

You would probably worry you would lose it.

Why?

Because in the end, you will lose every thing that is not

important

≈> Don't confuse yourself with things

Doing

I'd like to lead the best life possible

Great

But I don't know what to do

Don't start with doing, start with being

Being who?

Being who you are

≈> Get beyond doing and into the being

Money

I'd like more money

Why?

Then I would feel good

Try feeling good anyway

How do I do that?

Have you ever felt good?

≈> Happiness comes from not wanting

Life

What should I do with my life?

Who determines "should"?

What shall I do with my life?

Indeed, what shall you do?

You tell me

There's no-one else, it's your call

≈> And now it's time for your response

Looking

I am looking for happiness

Where have you looked?

Everywhere

You're looking in the wrong place

Where can I look?

Look every-when, look in every moment

≈> Happiness is not in the world. It's in here

Happiness

Where is happiness?

Inside you and me and everyone

But the causes of happiness are outside

Only when they are your focus, and they fade in an instant

≈> Happiness is inside trying to get out

Fame

I want to be famous

Why?

So many people will think I'm good

Do you think you're good?

I'm not sure

Whose opinion will you go with?

≈> Other's views matter only as they influence your own.

Needing

I need you

Can you have me?

No, you're you, I'm me

So how could you need me?

I feel like I need you to be complete

Be whole

≈> Possessing others would be slavery: choose their freedom

and yours

Lots

I need lots of things

You don't need what you don't have

How come?

Because you are OK as you are

≈> What you don't have you don't need for this moment,

or this one.

Possessions

I want more possessions

Then you will hang on to them

What's the alternative?

Let go, even of those you look after

What's good about that?

You'll be ready to lose everything

≈> Trying to grip what you will lose creates anxiety

Breathe

What must I do?

Breathe?

There must be more to it than that?

Breathe deeply

That's it?

And diaphragmatically

≈> Deep breathing ushers in deeper awareness

Better

I want more money

Why would you want more than others?

I'd feel better about myself

And why do you need to do that?

Because I don't feel so good

Do you know why you want more?

≈> Stop wanting, start enjoying

Nothing

What must I have?

There is nothing you must have

What must I do?

There is nothing you must do

What must I be?

You already are

≈> Do nothing and be in touch with everything

The Cause

Order

How can I get my life in order?

Why not when?

OK, when can I?

Start now

How?

Create some order in your mind

≈> Life is an inside out process.

Worry

I worry about the world

The worry is your problem

If I stop worrying it will get better?

It will stop making it worse

≈> Our worries come out to meet us; cancel the order!

Expect

How are you?

Not too bad

What do you expect of life?

Not too much

Then that's what you will tend to get

≈> Your expectations keep turning up. Turn up your expectations.

Wants

What do you really want?

I don't know

Who else could?

Just me

If you don't know, will you get it?

Probably not

≈> Knowing what you want is the key

Process

How can I have more?

To have more, do more

But how can I do more?

Be more

How can I be more?

Come to your senses

≈> Sense, be, do and have, in that order

Pitch

Do I have free will?

What's the sound of an approaching train?

Maybe DOOO

What sound does it make as it moves away?

Maybe DAAA

So what was the sound?

≈> In the moment you have choice. Afterwards you didn't.

Physics

What about death?

What's the 1ˢᵗ rule of physics?

Energy/matter is never created or destroyed, it just changes form

And what are you?

Consciousness

And the 1ˢᵗ rule of consciousness is?

≈> Consciousness is never created or destroyed, it changes form

Rubbish

There's a lot of rubbish in my brain

Like what?

I'm no good, what I can't do

Good

Good?

It's good to notice that it's rubbish

≈> Notice habits you want to lose and then gradually

let go of them

Free

I don't know what to do

Would you like to obey my orders?

No

Would you like to be free?

Yes, I'd like to be free

Free of what

≈> You are free save for the convincing illusion you are not

Thoughts

Have you ever thought?

Thought what?

How thoughts get into your mind

Like that one?

And what you are thinking now

≈> Notice that you are the noticer.

Can't

I can't find what I'm looking for

Save yourself time, don't look

But how will I find it?

You just said you can't, rest

OK, I can

≈> Thoughts are seeds of deeds

Stupid

I'm unbelievably stupid

OK, believe it

You agree I'm stupid?

Have you made up your mind?

No

Neither have I

≈> Unconscious follows programming. To change yourself,

change your programming

Fate

It's just fate

What is?

What happens, it's just fate

Is it your fate to believe it's just fate?

Yes

What if it weren't?

≈> We are always future-creating

Decision

How can I determine my future?

Determine that you will determine it

And how will I do that?

Make the decision

How will I find out this works?

By living it

≈> You are living out your expectations

Change

I must change my life

Why is that?

Because I'm unhappy

And why are you unhappy?

I don't know

≈> The problem remains as you focus on how you don't

want it to be

Mood

Things get me down

Is that what you want them to do?

No, but they always do

When do you want them to build you up?

≈> Choose it, see it, feel it, be in it

Here

My life's going nowhere

Where are you now?

Here

Where could you be tomorrow?

≈> If you don't know where you are going, you are

going nowhere

Fears

I hoped things would be better than this

But you feared they would be worse?

Yes

So you got what you expected

How?

You got the average

≈> Hopes and fears radiate creatively

Miracles

I'd like to perform miracles

Try making your heart beat

I don't have to try

That's a miracle

≈> You are a miracle within a miracle

Meant

How's it going?

All is well

Everything?

Everything is as it's meant to be

Who meant it?

You did, we all did, now it's turned up

≈> Whatever you meant to be will be

Light

I want to do the right thing

Don't try to do what is right

Why not?

They are changing constructs

Then we are lost

Instead do what is light

≈> You can feel what feels light

Drama and World

Negative

I'm not happy with who I am

That's good

Why?

If you're not happy, you'll want to change

≈> Use unhappiness as a spur to happiness

Change

I want to change the world

There is a way

What is it?

Change yourself

Are you sure you want to know

≈> You are your territory

Exceptions

So many bad things happen in the world

How do you know?

I watch the news

What happened to you?

Well I'm OK

When you are OK, you think of bad things?

≈> News is news because it is an exception to the truth

Experience

There's a lot of bad news in the world

Really?

I read of deaths every day

And they're true?

Yes

Did you get killed yesterday?

≈> Millions leave the world every day and millions more come:

what will you do while you are here?

Place

My friend takes drugs

Why?

She's looking for something else

That's good, has she found it?

No, not yet

Because she's looking in the wrong place

≈> Drugs are diversions from a better path

Sleep

What happens to me when I sleep?

You dream

What happens to me when I'm awake?

You dream

How do you mean?

After this life, you wake

≈> The challenge is to wake up while you are here

Bad

How are you?

Not too bad

Just a bit better than too bad

Wouldn't you prefer to feel great?

Yes

Start practicing

≈> It's too bad if you're not-too-bad

If

If I had enough I'd be OK

How come?

Then I'd do what I want and be who I want to be

Why not take a shortcut?

How do I do that?

Don't wait to have or do, simply be

≈> It's not OK for it not to be OK now

Race

What does the human race need to know?

That it's not a race

What do you mean?

There is nowhere to go

Really?

Only now here to be

≈> Stop running and let it be

Love

I'd like more love in the world

That's easy

How?

Be more loving

And how do I do that?

Make the time to feel love and send it out

≈> You are always radiating who you are

Awake

The world is waking up

Is it morning?

People are waking up all over the world

Why?

They have realized they don't know

≈> Recognizing ignorance is a great start

Suffering

Why do people suffer?

They'll know what it is like

To suffer?

And what is it like not to suffer

≈> Every thing is temporary, you are real

Anger

I'm mad about what happened

Does that feel good?

No it feels bad, but it shouldn't have happened

So you want to punish yourself?

≈> Anger is a self-inflicting punishment

Dwell

I'd like to be happy now

Be happy

How?

Dwell on it

≈> To know you must see the stillness, to see the stillness you

must be still

Control

I don't have control

Who controls the world?

No-one

Who controls themselves?

No-one?

Start with yourself and ripple outwards

≈> The first step to self-control is awareness that you don't have

it

Deep listening

Positive

I like to pray

How do you pray?

I say words

Prayer is energy, the words are incidental

Really?

Make sure the energy is positive

≈> Intend to influence the energy you emit

Prophet

Why won't God speak to me?

Has God ever spoken to anyone?

Yes, he spoke to the prophets

But he's not speaking now?

No

Why, did God get bored?

≈> If you are not fully here, you won't hear

Faith

I have faith

What is faith?

I'm not sure

Then you don't have faith

≈> Develop your intent muscles

In

I believe in God

What do you mean by "in"?

Eh?

Are you in God?

I don't know

Are you outside?

≈> Be aware of where you are

Arctic

I don't believe there's a God

Have you been to the Arctic circle?

No

Do you believe it exists?

Yes

Why?

⇝ You don't know what you don't know

Works

I believe in God

Why not believe in you?

I prefer God

Who created you?

God

So you believe in you

≈> Know the fruit and then the tree

Disappoint

I disappointed God

Does God know everything?

Yes

Then God cannot be disappointed

≈> The knower cannot be disappointed

Hell

I worry about hell

Do you love anyone?

Yes

Would your God love them too?

Much more

Would you ever send them to hell?

≈> A loving God would not choose to be unloving

Made

What if we make God send us to hell?

Is God all-powerful?

Yes

Could we make God do anything?

≈> The all-powerful would always be all-powerful

Belief

Is there a God?

How would you know?

I don't know, you tell me

Would you believe me?

Probably not

≈> People talk about God who don't know God

Devil

Why did God create the devil?

Why would God do that?

To tempt us

And why would he do that?

To find out if we are good enough

Doesn't he already know?

≈> An all-knowing God has nothing to know

Complete

I must praise God

Why

God needs our praise

Is God complete?

Yes

Then God needs nothing from us

≈> Almost nothing is needed any now

Church

I've got to go to church

Which one?

The one I believe in

But what about the others

My one is the right one

How do you know?

≈> The next point on your path is always calling you.

Says

I believe in God

What does she say?

I don't know

Why do you believe her?

≈> Do not believe what you do not experience

Listen

God never listens to me

How do you know?

He never replies

You haven't heard her?

Not a single word

Listen to the breeze

≈> No-one is heard when no-one listens

Religions

Don't religions help?

Religions help and hinder

How so?

Each religion's founder points to the truth

Wouldn't that help?

But the followers look at the founder instead

≈> See the truth, be the truth

Guidance

There is no guidance

How do you know?

I haven't experienced guidance

How much have you asked for?

≈> You don't get what you don't ask for

Acknowledgement

My friends Jefferson Cann, Vaughn Malcolm and Sarah Singleton kindly reviewed these thoughts and gently challenged me. Thank you, amazing people.

B O O K S

O is a symbol of the world, of oneness and unity. In different cultures it also means the "eye," symbolizing knowledge and insight. We aim to publish books that are accessible, constructive and that challenge accepted opinion, both that of academia and the "moral majority."

Our books are available in all good English language bookstores worldwide. If you don't see the book on the shelves ask the bookstore to order it for you, quoting the ISBN number and title. Alternatively you can order online (all major online retail sites carry our titles) or contact the distributor in the relevant country, listed on the copyright page.

See our website www.o-books.net for a full list of over 500 titles, growing by 100 a year.

And tune in to myspiritradio.com for our book review radio show, hosted by June-Elleni Laine, where you can listen to the authors discussing their books.

MySpiritRadio